I0413268

Preliminary Analysis of Greater Sage-Grouse Reproduction in the Virginia Mountains of Northwestern Nevada

By Peter S. Coates, Zachary B. Lockyer, Melissa A. Farinha, Joelle M. Sweeney, Valerie M. Johnson, and Matthew G. Meshriy, U.S. Geological Survey; Shawn P. Espinosa, Nevada Department of Wildlife; David J. Delehanty, Idaho State University, and Michael L. Casazza, U.S. Geological Survey

Prepared in cooperation with the Nevada Department of Wildlife, Idaho State University, and the U.S. Fish and Wildlife Service

Open-File Report 2011–1182

U.S. Department of the Interior
U.S. Geological Survey

U.S. Department of the Interior
KEN SALAZAR, Secretary

U.S. Geological Survey
Marcia K. McNutt, Director

U.S. Geological Survey, Reston, Virginia: 2011

For more information on the USGS—the Federal source for science about the Earth, its natural and living resources, natural hazards, and the environment, visit http://www.usgs.gov or call 1-888-ASK-USGS.

For an overview of USGS information products, including maps, imagery, and publications, visit http://www.usgs.gov/pubprod

To order this and other USGS information products, visit *http://store.usgs.gov*

Contents

Abstract 1

Project Overview 1

Study Area 2

Methods 2

    Monitoring Sage-Grouse 2

        Capturing and Handling 2

        Radio-Telemetry 3

        Space-Use 3

        Nest Videography 4

        Nest Vegetation Measurements, Nest Site Selection, and Nest Success 4

        Brood Monitoring 5

        Brood Vegetation Measurements 5

        Modeling Habitat Selection and Nest Survival 5

    Predator Monitoring 6

        Raven and Raptor Surveys 6

        Raven Videography 6

        Badger Surveys 6

Preliminary Results 7

    Radio-Telemetry 7

    Space-Use 8

    Nest Survival 12

    Selection of Nesting Habitat 14

    Sage-Grouse Nest Videography 20

    Brood Success 23

    Selection of Brood-Rearing Habitat 24

    Predator Surveys 27

Preliminary Data Interpretation 29

Acknowledgments 30

Literature Cited 31

Figures

Figure 1. Locations of radio-marked sage-grouse in the Virginia Mountains of Nevada 8

Figure 2. Utilization distribution of sage-grouse in the Virginia Mountains of Nevada. 9

Figure 3. Utilization distribution of brood-rearing sage-grouse in the Virginia Mountains of Nevada during 2010 10

Figure 4. Home ranges (95 percent utilization distribution) of individual sage-grouse in the Virginia Mountains of Nevada during the reproductive period 11

Figure 5. The average home range (95 percent utilization distribution) of adult and yearling sage-grouse in the Virginia Mountain. 12

Figure 6. Successful and unsuccessful nests of sage-grouse in the Virginia Mountains 13

Figure 7. Mean values (bars represent standard errors) for percentages of understory cover at locations of failed and successful nests of sage-grouse in the Virginia Mountains of Nevada during 2009 and 2010 14

Figure 8. Frequency of use of overhead cover type of sage-grouse nests in the Virginia Mountains during 2009 and 2010 16

Figure 9. Mean values (lines represent standard errors) of percentages of cover by shrub types at 5, 10, 25, 50, and 100-m distances from nest sites and random locations 18

Figure 10. Mean values (lines represent standard errors) of percentages of cover by perennial grass and cheatgrass (*Bromus tectorum*) at nest sites compared to dependent and independent random points 19

Figure 11. Mean values (lines represent standard errors) for percentages of cover by perennial and annual forbs at nest sites, nest-dependent random points, and nest-independent random points in the Virginia Mountains during 2009 and 2010 20

Figure 12. Images of nest activities at eight sage-grouse nests and one raven nest in the Virginia Mountains of northwestern Nevada during 2009 and 2010 22

Figure 13. Frequency of documented encounters of species at sage-grouse nests in the Virginia Mountains during 2009 and 2010 22

Figure 14. Sequence of still photographs from video recordings of a raven attacking a female sage-grouse and depredating the eggs within an 8-second period. 23

Figure 15. Mean values for percentages of cover types used by brood-rearing female sage-grouse and cover types found at brood-dependent random points 24

Figure 16. Mean values of percentages of vertical and overall cover for brood locations and brood-dependent random locations. 25

Figure 17. Percentages of cover (lines represent standard errors of the means) at day-nesting, night-nesting, and brood-dependent random locations over the 50-day post-hatch interval for sage-grouse in the Virginia Mountains during 2009 and 2010 26

Figure 18. Distribution of point surveys for ravens and raptors across the study areas in the Virginia Mountains of Nevada during 2009 and 2010 28

Figure 19. Raven nests monitored in 2009 29

Tables

Table 1. Number of sage-grouse radio tracked in the Virginia Mountains of Nevada, monitored during 2009 and 2010 and listed by sex and age class 7

Table 2. Mean values for vegetation characteristics of shrub and litter depth at sage-grouse nests and random (dependent and independent of nest site) points in the Virginia Mountains of Nevada during 2009 and 2010 15

Conversion Factors

Multiply	By	To obtain
Length		
centimeter (cm)	0.3937	inch (in.)
meter (m)	3.281	foot (ft)
kilometer (km)	0.6214	mile (mi)
kilometer (km)	0.5400	mile, nautical (nmi)
meter (m)	1.094	yard (yd)
Area		
hectare (ha)	2.471	acre
square kilometer (km^2)	247.1	acre
hectare (ha)	0.003861	square mile (mi^2)
square kilometer (km^2)	0.3861	square mile (mi^2)
Mass		
kilogram (kg)	2.205	pound avoirdupois (lb)

Preliminary Analysis of Greater Sage-Grouse Reproduction in the Virginia Mountains of Northwestern Nevada

By Peter S. Coates, Zachary B. Lockyer, Melissa A. Farinha, Joelle M. Sweeney, Valerie M. Johnson, and Matthew G. Meshriy, U.S. Geological Survey; Shawn P. Espinosa, Nevada Department of Wildlife; David J. Delehanty, Idaho State University, and Michael L. Casazza, U.S. Geological Survey

Abstract

Relationships between habitat selection and population vital rates of greater sage-grouse (*Centrocercus urophasianus*; hereafter sage-grouse), recently designated as a candidate species under the Endangered Species Act, within the Great Basin are not well-understood. The growing development of renewable energy infrastructure within areas inhabited by sage-grouse is thought to influence predator and vegetation communities. For example, common ravens (*Corvus corax*), a synanthropic sage-grouse nest predator, are increasing range-wide and select transmission lines and other tall structures for nesting and perching. In the Virginia Mountains of northwestern Nevada, we collected preliminary information of space-use, habitat selection, and population vital rates during the nesting and brood-rearing period over two years on 56 sage-grouse. Additionally, videography at nest sites ($n = 22$) was used to identify sage-grouse nest predators. The study area is a potential site for renewable energy developments (i.e., wind and solar), and we plan to continue monitoring this population using a before-after-control-impact study design. The results reported here are preliminary and further data is required before conclusions can be drawn from this population of sage-grouse.

Project Overview

The U.S. Geological Survey (USGS), Nevada Department of Wildlife (NDOW), Idaho State University (ISU), and U.S. Fish and Wildlife Service collaborated on an intensive effort to monitor a population of Greater Sage-Grouse (*Centrocercus urophasianus*; hereafter sage-grouse) in the Virginia Mountains of northwestern Nevada. A portion of the study area is scheduled for development of wind energy and associated transmission infrastructure. Relatively little information is known regarding habitat and predator communities of sage-grouse within this area, and these factors may be influenced by anthropogenic subsidies. Regulatory agencies consider anthropogenic landscape alterations as potential threats to persistence of sage-grouse populations. Field biologists have initiated a before-after-control-impact (BACI) study design to investigate potential positive and negative effects of developments on population vital rates and habitat selection.

1

The purpose of this study was to collect and interpret empirical data before and after construction of energy infrastructure to estimate potential effects of threats to sage-grouse populations and habitat. This report contains summary data and preliminary findings of 2009 and 2010, which represent a portion of the preconstruction years of the ongoing study. It also describes some of our future planned efforts related to this study, with respect to monitoring and data analyses. This report presents preliminary findings on nest survival, brood survival, and space-use of sage-grouse during the reproductive period. Also presented are results of preliminary analyses to identify habitat characteristics selected by sage-grouse and factors that influence nest and brood survival. The preconstruction-phase findings presented in this report should be interpreted as only preliminary because sample sizes were limited.

Study Area

We captured sage-grouse at two lek (defined as a traditional breeding ground) locations in the Virginia Mountains during the spring and fall months of 2008–2010. The leks used for capture were the only two leks known to be active within the Virginia Mountains. One site was located at Sheep Springs, near Fish Springs Ranch on the north slope of the Virginia Mountains. The other was located approximately 14 kilometers (km) to the southeast on Spanish Flat, near Tule Peak. The overall study area encompassing both leks was approximately 652.7 square kilometers (km^2).

Dominant plant communities consisted of sagebrush (*Artemisia* spp.) steppe at lower elevations and mountain shrub at higher elevations. Overstory at lower elevations was primarily characterized by big sagebrush (*A. tridentata* spp.). Other shrub cover consisted of Bailey's greasewood (*Sarcobatus baileyi*), horsebrush (*Tetradymia* sp.), and a variety of rabbitbrush (*Chrysothamnus* spp.). Overstory of mountain shrub communities was characterized by big sagebrush and a variety of mountain shrubs, including Saskatoon serviceberry (*Amelanchier alnifolia*), snowberry (*Symphoricarpos albus*), and antelope bitterbrush (*Purshia tridentata*). Dominant forbs consisted of woolly mule's ear (*Wyethia mollis*), lupine (*lupines* spp.), and arrowleaf balsamroot (*Balsamorhiza sagittata*). Singleleaf pinyon (*Pinus monophylla*) and Utah Juniper (*Juniperus osteosperma*) woodlands occurred throughout the study area. Grasses included bluebunch wheatgrass (*Pseudorogeneria cristatum*), crested wheatgrass (*Agropyron cristatum*), Basin wildrye (*Leymus cinereus*), needle-and-thread grass (*Hesperostipa comata*) and Indian ricegrass (*Achnatherum hymenoides*). During 1999, a fire near Fish Springs Ranch, NV burned >84.8 km^2 of sagebrush steppe and mountain shrub communities. Although cheatgrass (*Bromus tectorum*) occurred throughout the study area, the invasive grass was most abundant in burned areas.

Methods

Monitoring Sage-Grouse

Capturing and Handling

We located sage-grouse after sunset and before sunrise with spotlights and used nets attached to 3-meter (m) extension handles (Wakkinen and others, 1992) and hand-held net-launching devices (SuperTalon®, Advanced Weapons Technology, La Quinta, Calif.) to capture sage-grouse. Birds were equipped with battery powered necklace-style radio transmitters (less than 3 percent body mass, weight of bird was 1–1.8 kilograms [kg]; Schroeder and others, 1999; Advanced Telemetry Systems, Isanti, Minn.). Sage-grouse were also weighed, and multiple length measurements, including tarsus and culmen, were recorded to generate a body condition index. Blood was extracted from the brachial vein for deoxyribonucleic acid (DNA) analyses. We determined age based on plumage (Ammann, 1944). During spring months, sage-grouse were classified as either adult (AD) or yearling (AHY). During fall months, sage-grouse were classified as AD or hatch-year (HY). Age classifications were based on plumage characteristics of the 9th and 10th primaries. Plumage photographs (including wings extended, retrices, as well as breast and head profile poses) were taken of each sage-grouse prior to release at its location of capture.

Radio-Telemetry

We monitored sage-grouse movement, survivorship, and reproduction following release throughout the spring and summer months (March 15 – 05 August). We used a 3-element Yagi antenna and portable receiver (Communication Specialist Inc. Orange, Calif.; Advanced Telemetry Inc., Isanti, Minn.) to track radio-marked sage-grouse, and we minimized relocation error by encircling each sage-grouse by using a 30–50 m buffer to pinpoint the bird's location. After pinpointing the bird being tracked, we approximated the distance and a compass bearing from a known location (recorded by using global positioning system [GPS] equipment) to obtain the location coordinates (Universal Transverse Mercator) of the bird's location. Throughout the nesting and brood-rearing periods, we attempted to locate female sage-grouse at least twice per week.

Space-Use

The coordinates of the relocation points were plotted into a geographical information system (GIS) (ArcGIS 9.2, ESRI Products, Redlands, Calif.) for space-use analysis. We conducted three analyses by using kernel density estimations for the spring and summer months. The kernel density estimates provide a measure of the utilization distribution (UD) of sage-grouse across the landscape (Worton, 1989). Thus, utilization distributions are useful to visualize where on the landscape sage-grouse were frequently relocated. In the first analysis, we calculated the amount of area within the upper 50 and 95 percent contours of the highest density region based on the entire relocation dataset (pooled across individuals). We considered the 50 percent contour as the core area and the 95 percent contour as home range. The purpose of using the pooled dataset was to estimate area used at the population level. The kernel density calculations were carried out in multiple steps. The relocation points were weighted to account for biases associated with nonequivalent relocation intervals. We calculated the smoothing parameters (*h*) by using least-squares cross validation in Animal Space Use 1.3 (Horne and Garton, 2009), which minimized the difference in volume between the true UD and the estimated UD. We imported those smoothing parameters into a GIS (ArcGIS 9.2) and used Hawth's Tools (Beyer, 2004) to calculate fixed kernel densities. Kernel density maps were generated based on the estimated densities for 2009 and 2010. In the second analysis, we calculated kernel density estimates for each individual sage-grouse by using the same steps described above. We only calculated estimates for an area within the upper 95 percent contour of the highest density for individuals. In the third analysis, we examined areas used by brood-rearing sage-grouse by calculating 95 percent kernel density estimates for only sage-grouse with broods during the brood-rearing period.

Nest Videography

When a radio-marked sage-grouse was found at the same location multiple times during the early nesting period, we visually determined if the sage-grouse was nesting (Coates and Delehanty, 2010). Nests were monitored ≥3 times per week until their fate was determined. Nests were classified as successful when one or more chicks hatched. Nests were also scored as depredated, partially depredated, or abandoned. In addition to monitoring nests with radio telemetry, we installed camouflaged microcameras with time-lapsed digital video recorders (DVR) on 6 and 16 nests during 2009 and 2010, respectively. The primary purpose of cameras was to identify nest predators (Holloran and Anderson, 2003; Coates and others, 2008). Another purpose was to identify factors that influence patterns of incubation (Coates and Delehanty, 2008). Cameras were placed approximately 0.5 m from the nest bowl, which aided in unambiguous identification of animal encounters and sage-grouse behavior. Cameras and video recorders were uninstalled immediately following nest predation, abandonment, or hatch. We sought to reduce human scent by wearing rubberized gloves and using spray designed to mask scent.

Nest Vegetation Measurements, Nest Site Selection, and Nest Success

Following nest fate, we recorded understory cover at the nest bowl by using three techniques, including a coverboard (modified from Jones, 1968), a Robel pole (Robel and others, 1970), and a digital photographic method. The purpose of using three techniques was to compare the results obtained by each method. Measurements using a cover board were conducted at 2-m from the point and 0, 45, and 90 degree angles from the ground. We categorized vertical cover as measurements at 0 and 45 degree angles and overall cover as those at all three angles. We also measured composition of vegetation cover at five subplots (20 × 50 centimeters [cm]) located ≤25 m of each nest by using the Daubenmire method (Daubenmire, 1959). After randomizing the orientation of the quadrant, we measured canopy cover along two 25-m transects, one 50-m transect, and one 100-m transect, all extending from the nest bowl at 90° intervals. We recorded shrub species and measured and recorded width (cm) and heights (cm) of a random sample of individual shrubs along the line. These shrub widths were measured within 5, 10, and 25 m from the nest for all four transect lines, within 50 m for two transect lines, and 100 m for one transect line. The purpose of the different transect lengths was to identify the scale where selection for shrub cover occurs at nest sites. We also used a GIS to measure multiple explanatory variables within the landscape (ArcGIS, ESRI software, Redlands, CA). We classified features across the study areas as multiple dominant cover types, including sagebrush steppe shrubland, riparian, meadow, agriculture, perennial grassland, annual grassland, sagebrush steppe interspersed with pinyon-juniper woodlands, and pinyon-juniper woodland.

To examine nest site habitat selection, defined as habitat use disproportionate to availability (Hall and others, 1997), we compared means and variance of measurements of vegetation characteristics at nests to those at random points. To characterize available habitat, we generated random points throughout the study site and conducted the same habitat measurements at those locations centered at the nearest shrub. Habitat characteristics at random locations were then compared to those at nest locations. We evaluated evidence for multi-scale selection by generating two random points for each nest. One point was within 500 m of the nest (dependent random point) and the other was within the study area (independent random point). The preliminary results were reported as means (± standard error of the mean [SE]) of vegetation characteristics for random points and nests.

Nests were scored as successful if ≥1 egg hatched. We estimated daily nest survival parameters using maximum likelihood procedures in Program R with the package RMark (Laake and Rexstad 1999). We report apparent nest success and maximum likelihood derived survival rates.

Brood Monitoring

Following the completion of a successful nest, we obtained locations of monitored radio-collared female sage-grouse with broods two or more times per week. Every 10 days following nest hatch, we used spotlights during night surveys to count the number of chicks in each brood. To confirm an unsuccessful brood (and prevent a false negative), females were re-spotlighted for brood presence within 48 hours of finding a female with no brood.

Brood Vegetation Measurements

We conducted a similar habitat measurement protocol at brood sites as was conducted at nest sites; however, maximum extent of the transect line was 25 m for brood sites. To determine exact brood locations for habitat measurements, the exact point of the resting female sage-grouse was recorded with a photograph or the distance and direction were noted from a distinct feature on the landscape in the immediate area of the sage-grouse. Canopy cover was measured along three 25-m transects extending from the brood location every 120°, with random orientation. We measured the width (cm) of each shrub species along the three transect lines within 5, 10, and 25 m from the brood location. Because habitat changes through time and broods are mobile, we conducted measurements at each 10-day interval. We also investigated differences in vegetation use between night (roosting) and day (foraging) hours. These surveys included one day and one night observation of habitat used by females with broods (within a 24-hour period), as well as one observation of a random location within 850 m of the brood (dependent) to estimate disproportionate use to availability.

Modeling Habitat Selection and Nest Survival

We plan to extend these survival and selection analyses into a modeling framework after obtaining greater sample sizes (Casazza and others, in press). For example, generalized mixed-effects models at different spatial scales (that is, grain and extent) will be developed and evidence for models will be evaluated for habitat selection and survival of nests and broods. We chose explanatory variables (e.g., vegetation type) for each dependent variable to include in the models based on *a priori* information that represents competing hypotheses about habitat selection and survival. Resource selection functions (RSF) will be calculated from the used-available data (Manly and others, 2002) using model parameter estimates during the nesting and brood-rearing period. The RSF approximates the probability that a resource of type x_i is selected once it is encountered and provides a valuable measure of relative selection between resources of different types. We plan to use multiple parametric link functions (e.g., exponential and logistic) to identify the model that best describes the data. Random effects will be fit where we find evidence of support within the models to represent spatial and temporal correlation between sample units. We will use an information-theoretic approach (Anderson, 2008), including the [Delta] Akaike information criterion (ΔAIC) measure, Akaike's weights, and evidence ratios. We will also apply likelihood-based coefficient of determination (R^2) values and likelihood ratio tests to evaluate evidence between the competing *a priori* models. We will average parameter estimates across models to identify factors that influence selection and survival.

Predator Monitoring

Raven and Raptor Surveys

Because ravens are known to be an effective sage-grouse nest predator (Coates and others, 2008; Bui and others, 2010; Coates and Delehanty, 2010), and raptors are known to consume sage-grouse (Moynahan and others, 2006), we conducted surveys for Common Ravens (*Corvus corax*; hereafter ravens) and raptors during sage-grouse nesting and immediately following determination of nest fate. We conducted visual surveys (using binoculars) for each sage-grouse nest location from a distance of approximately 50–100 m from the incubating female. Surveys were conducted over a 15-minute period wherein all four cardinal directional quadrants around the nest were searched for equal time allotments. Time of sighting, bearing, and distance (estimated by using a rangefinder) of each raptor and raven was tallied and identified to species when possible.

We plan to model factors that influence raven and raptor population numbers, particularly in relation to energy infrastructure, using surveys that were conducted at random locations across the study area following data collection after energy development. Randomization of survey points across the study area will be critical in assessing impacts to sage-grouse populations. Points were generated both on and off undeveloped roads. Surveys were completed between mid-May and late-July. Surveys were carried out between one half hour before sunrise and one half hour following sunset. The same protocol for nest surveys was carried out at random survey points. Point surveys randomized within the study area will be used to estimate raven and raptor densities by using Program Distance (Thomas and others, 2010) across the landscape.

Raven Videography

We collected additional observational data on raven nests by using videography within the study area. The objectives for using videography included: (1) to investigate links between raven foraging activities and sage-grouse incubation patterns, (2) to estimate provisioning rates of raven nestlings, and (3) to identify components of the raven nestling diet. We plan to investigate differences between nests in anthropogenic and natural nesting substrates. Information gathered in this study will assist with future implementation techniques for wildlife management concerning raven and sage-grouse interactions. This information may be particularly useful in areas of energy development because ravens are often associated with anthropogenic resource subsidies, such as transmission towers and lines (Boarman, 2003; Bui and others, 2010).

Badger Surveys

Following the fate of the nest (hatched, abandoned, or depredated) and the sage-grouse had departed the nest site, we conducted surveys for American badger (*Taxidea taxus*; hereafter badger). We inspected a 4-m wide transect line that formed a bowtie pattern centered on the nest bowl. The total searching distance was 680 m. Badger surveys were conducted at all nest, dependent, and independent random points. Within each of the survey lines we detected and recorded fresh, intact badger holes; collapsed holes; small digs or scrapes; badger scat; or tracks. These measurements were used to develop a badger activity index.

Preliminary Results

Radio-Telemetry

Fifty-six sage-grouse were fitted with radio-transmitting collars from fall 2008 through June 2010 (table 1). In 2009, 24 female and 5 male sage-grouse were tracked by radio telemetry. In 2010, 23 female and 4 male sage-grouse were tracked. Three replacement collars were deployed during 2010 on sage-grouse captured during the fall of 2008. Most sage-grouse were relocated in the Spanish Flat area (fig. 1).

Table 1. Number of sage-grouse radio tracked in the Virginia Mountains of Nevada, monitored during 2009 and 2010 and listed by sex and age class.

Sex	Age	2009	2010
Males	Adult	4	1
	Yearling	1	3
Females	Adult	18	12
	Yearling	6	11
Total		29	27

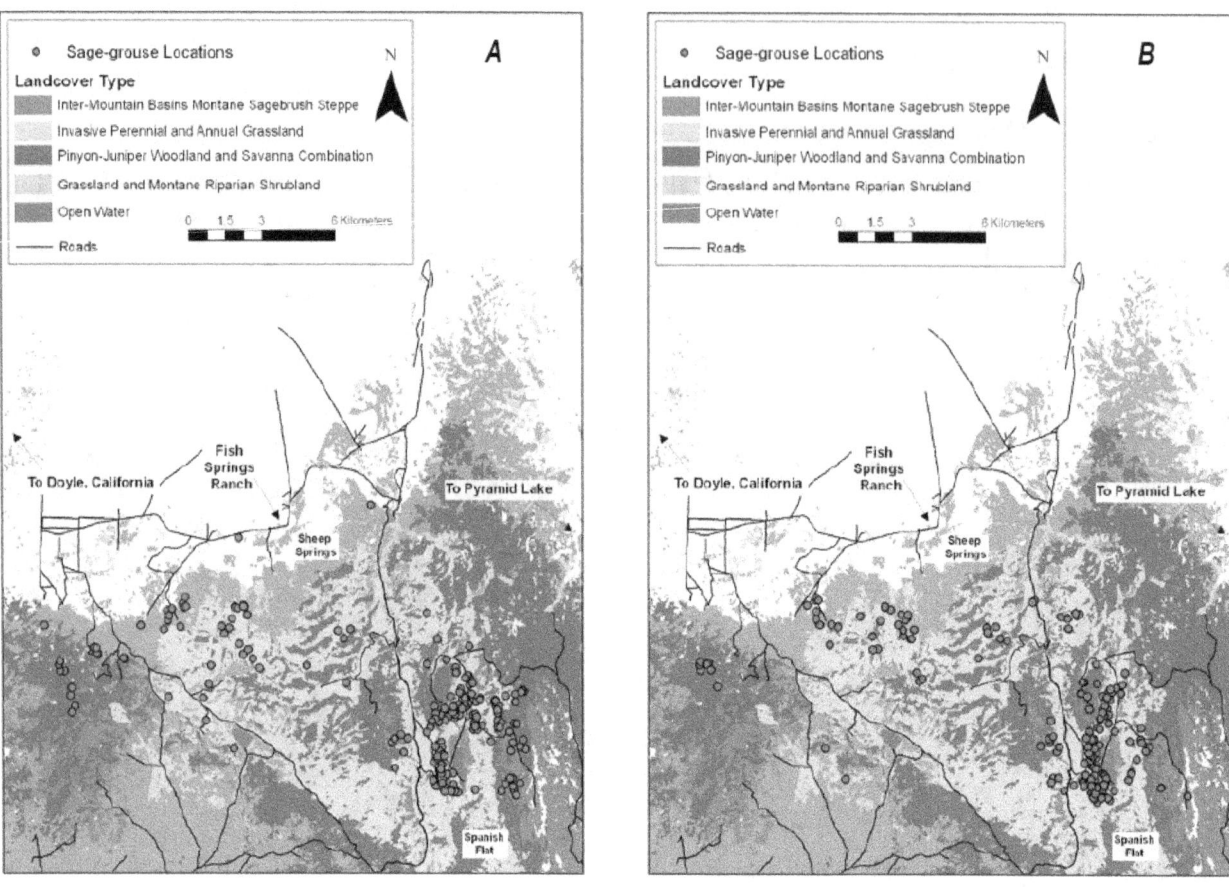

Figure 1. Locations of radio-marked sage-grouse in the Virginia Mountains of Nevada. *A*, During 2009. *B*, During 2010.

Space-Use

During 2009, the core area of sage-grouse activity (50 percent UD) was 2,320 hectares (ha) (fig. 2) according to pooled radio-location points. The home range (95 percent UD) at the population level encompassed 17,650 ha. During 2010, the core area was 1,930 ha, and the population-level home range encompassed 13,180 ha. In both years, the core area was located at Spanish Flat. Following successful nesting, brood-rearing females and male sage-grouse from both lek sites used this area before moving to wintering areas. In 2010, the core area of only brood-rearing sage-grouse was 700 ha, with a home range of 2,600 ha (fig. 3). The majority of individual home ranges throughout spring and summer overlapped within the Spanish Flat area, resulting in much less use of the Sheep Springs area (fig. 4), relatively speaking. Average home range size for individual sage-grouse was 2,470 ha ± 370 ha. Adult home range (2,870 ± 515 ha) was substantially greater than AHY (1,620 ha ± 300 ha), most notably in 2010 (fig. 5).

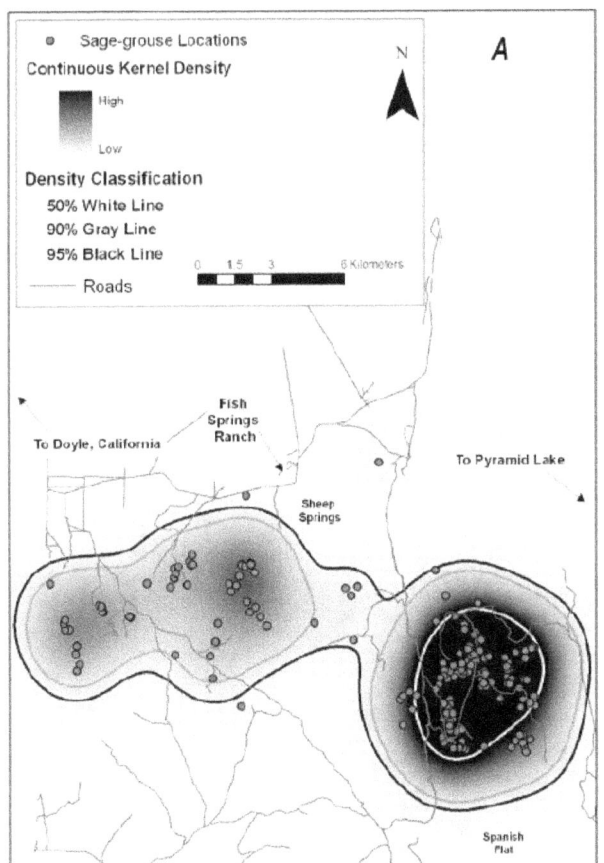
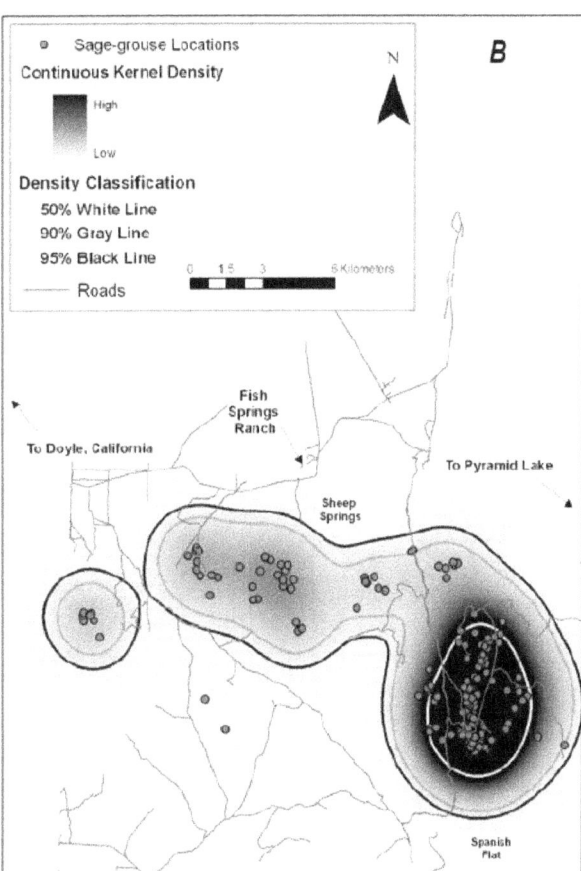

Figure 2. Utilization distribution of sage-grouse in the Virginia Mountains of Nevada. *A*, During 2009. *B*, During 2010. (Utilization distribution was approximated by using kernel density estimators).

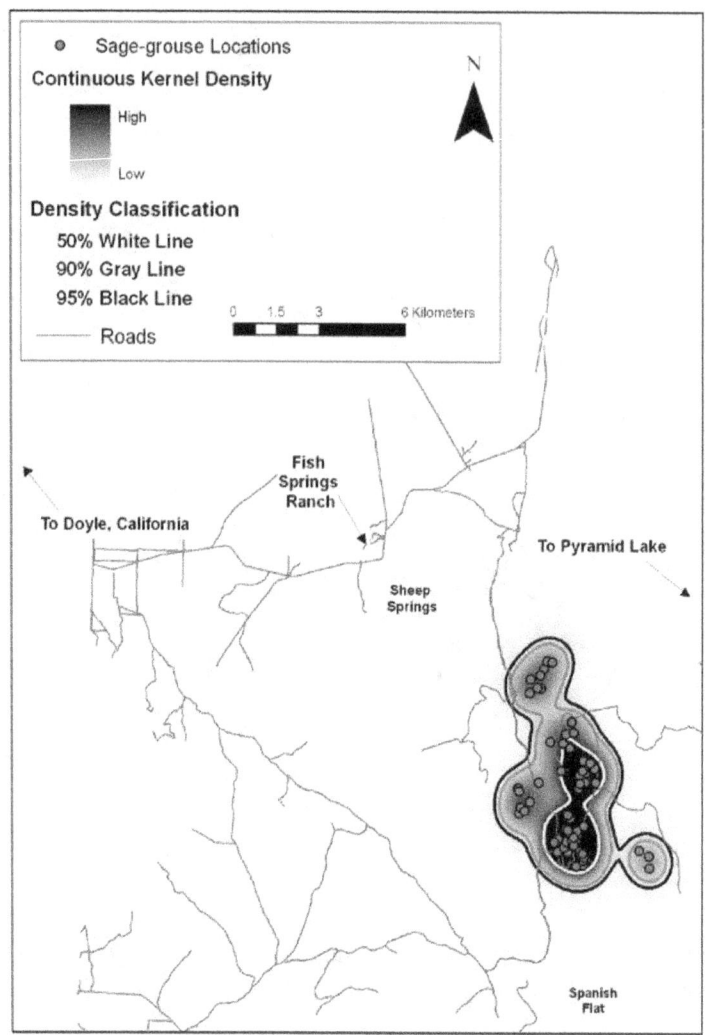

Figure 3. Utilization distribution of brood-rearing sage-grouse in the Virginia Mountains of Nevada during 2010. (Utilization distribution was approximated by using kernel density estimators).

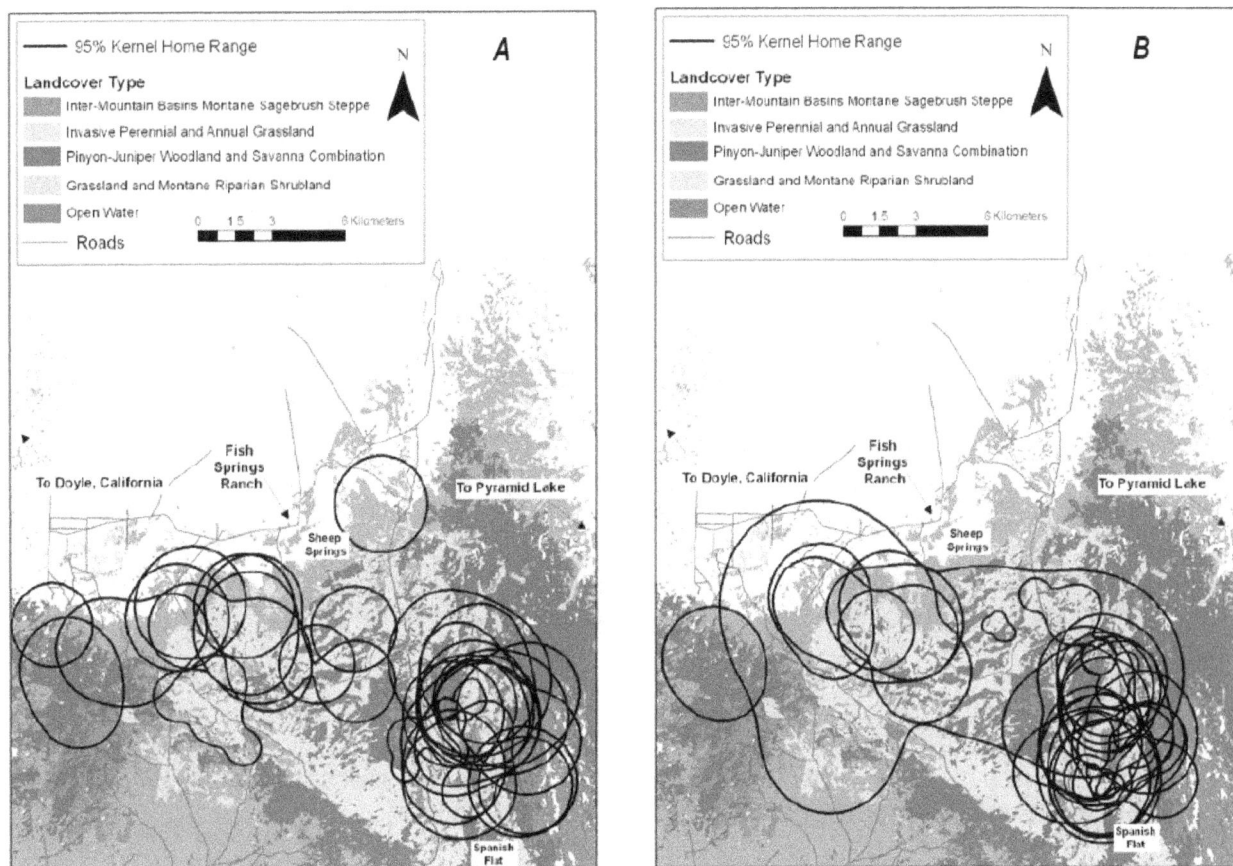

Figure 4. Home ranges (95 percent utilization distribution) of individual sage-grouse in the Virginia Mountains of Nevada during the reproductive period. *A*, In 2009. *B*, In 2010.

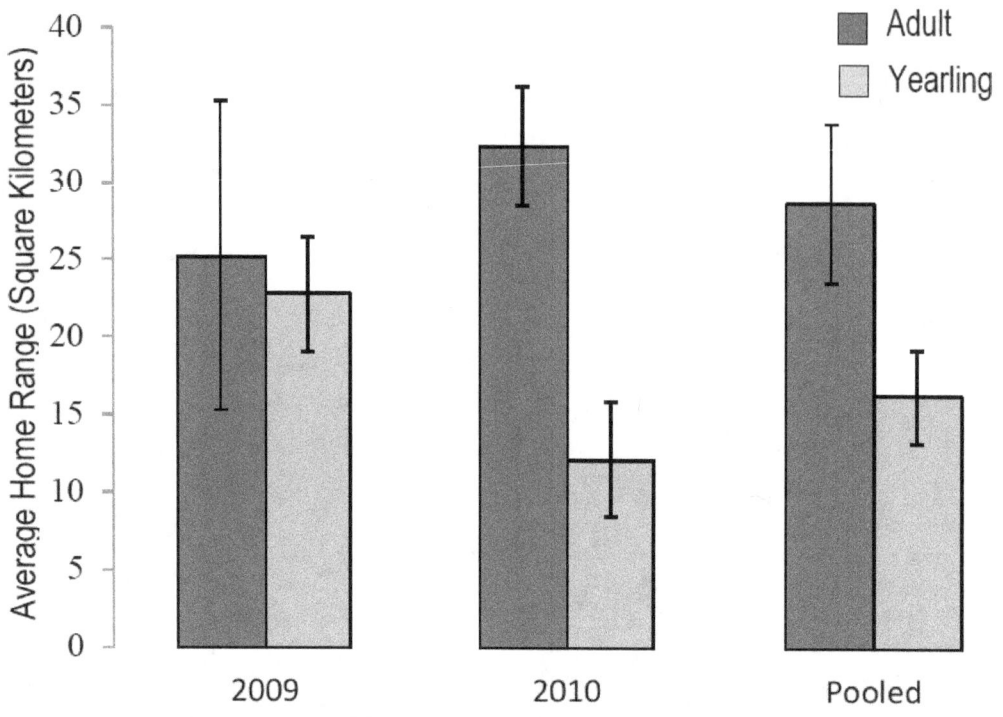

Figure 5. The average home range (95 percent utilization distribution) of adult and yearling sage-grouse in the Virginia Mountains (shown for 2009, 2010, and pooled [averaged across years]).

Nest Survival

We monitored 39 sage-grouse nests during 2009 and 2010 (fig. 6). Based on maximum likelihood estimation, nest survival was 13.5 percent (Confidence Interval; 8.9–20.2 percent) with a 37-day exposure period (laying and incubating). The estimated daily survival rate was 94.7 ± 1.1 percent. We documented 12 successful nests (first nest attempt = 9, second attempt = 3) and 27 failed nests (first = 25, second = 2), of which 24 were depredated (first =22, second = 2) and 3 first nests were abandoned. Two nests were partially depredated, but hatched 1 chick or more. One female died before nesting and another female slipped her radio-collar and we were unable to find her throughout the remainder of the season. Furthermore, signals were lost on three female sage-grouse during the nesting period, perhaps because of radio failure or movement away from the study region. The remaining radio-collared female sage-grouse did not attempt to nest, or nests were depredated prior to researcher detection (during the laying period). We did not document third nesting attempts.

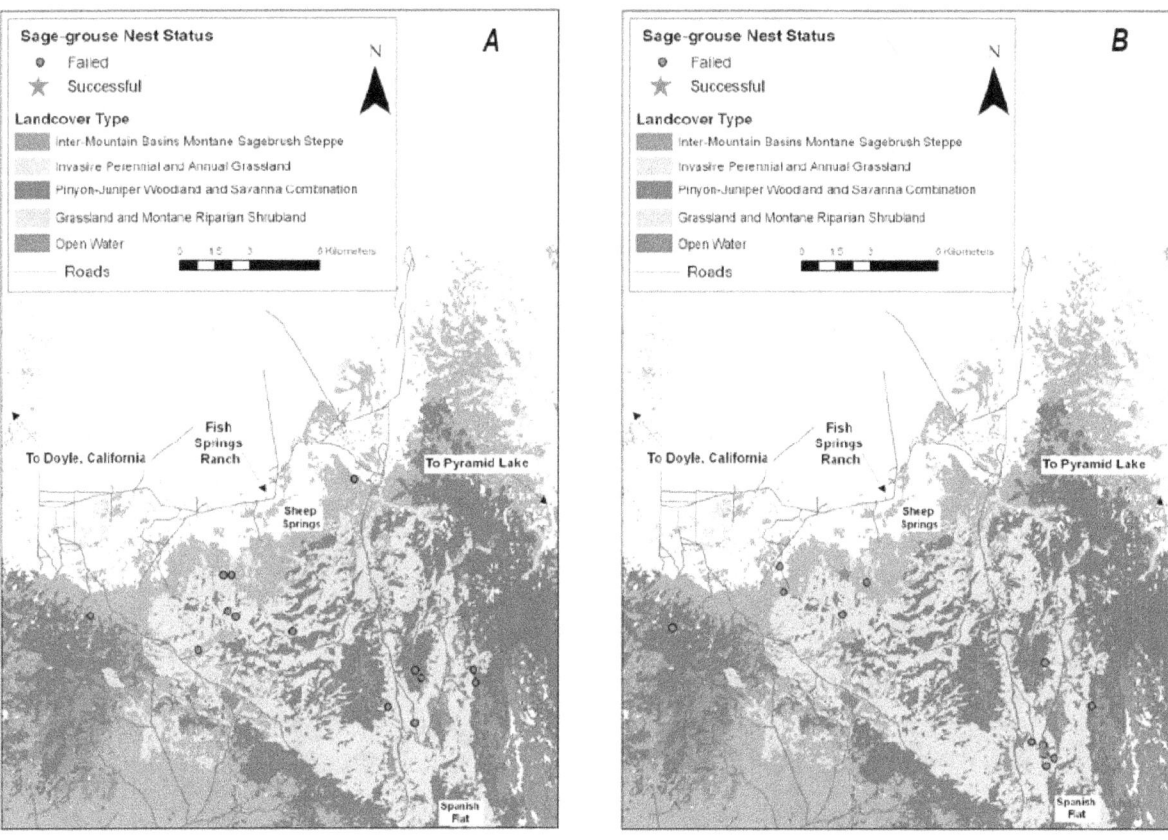

Figure 6. Successful and unsuccessful nests of sage-grouse in the Virginia Mountains. *A*, During 2009. *B*, During 2010.

On average, we measured greater vegetation understory cover by using the coverboard at successful nests (52.5 ± 2.7 percent) than at unsuccessful nests (41.0 ± 2.3 percent; fig. 7). Nest vegetation cover is currently being analyzed using the photographic method. We plan to compare results between field methodologies. We did not detect any other microhabitat factors important to nest survival. Preliminary results generated using a GIS suggested that unsuccessful nests were generally associated with greater areas of invasive grassland vegetation types, mostly consisting of cheatgrass (*Bromus tectorum*); however, additional data and analyses are needed to fully understand microhabitat and landscape factors that explain variation in nest survival (for example, canopy cover, cover type, and the number of predators). Nest locations ranged in elevation from approximately 1,500 to 2,100 m. During the final analyses of the study, we plan to include environmental covariates, such as vegetation measurements and time-dependent effects, into sage-grouse nest survival models.

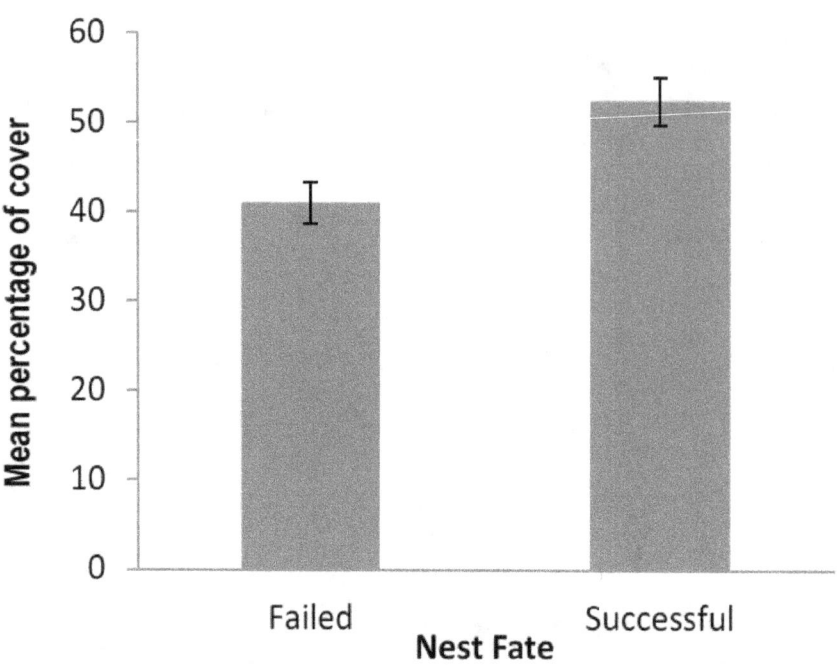

Figure 7. Mean values (bars represent standard errors) for percentages of understory cover at locations of failed and successful nests of sage-grouse in the Virginia Mountains of Nevada during 2009 and 2010.

Selection of Nesting Habitat

Nests were nearly always located under the canopy of shrub vegetation. The maximum height of nest shrubs averaged across nests was 76.1 ± 4.4 cm (range, 50–129 cm). The greatest width of nest shrubs averaged 117.5 ± 5.8 cm (83–170 cm), and the perpendicular width averaged 88.1 ± 5.1 cm (51–150 cm). The base of nests was comprised of litter placed on the ground. The average depth of the litter was 2.3 ± 0.2 cm (1–4 cm). Our preliminary findings suggest nest shrubs had greater height and width than shrubs measured at random dependent locations (table 2); however, we did not find a difference in shrub height and width at nest sites and random independent points. These preliminary findings indicate that sage-grouse are selecting nest shrubs with greater heights and widths within the immediate area (or on a local scale) (500 m from nest) only.

Females nested underneath the canopy of numerous shrub species, and one female was found nesting under a rock outcrop (fig. 8). The most frequently used shrubs were sagebrush (25 percent) and rabbitbrush (20 percent). Other vegetation included Bailey's greasewood, horsebrush, rabbitbrush, serviceberry, snowberry, and Great Basin wildrye.

Table 2. Mean values for vegetation characteristics of shrub and litter depth at sage-grouse nests and random (dependent and independent of nest site) points in the Virginia Mountains of Nevada during 2009 and 2010.

[Numbers in parentheses represent standard errors of the means; D, dependent of nest site; I, independent of nest site]

Point	Greatest height (cm)	Greatest width (cm)	Perpendicular width (cm)	Litter depth (cm)
Nest	76.1 (4.4)	117.5 (5.8)	88.1 (5.1)	2.3 (0.2)
Random (D)	64.4 (4.7)	104.0 (9.0)	82.4 (7.2)	1.6 (0.5)
Random (I)	75.5 (2.8)	114.1 (6.7)	89.5 (5.0)	2.7 (0.5)

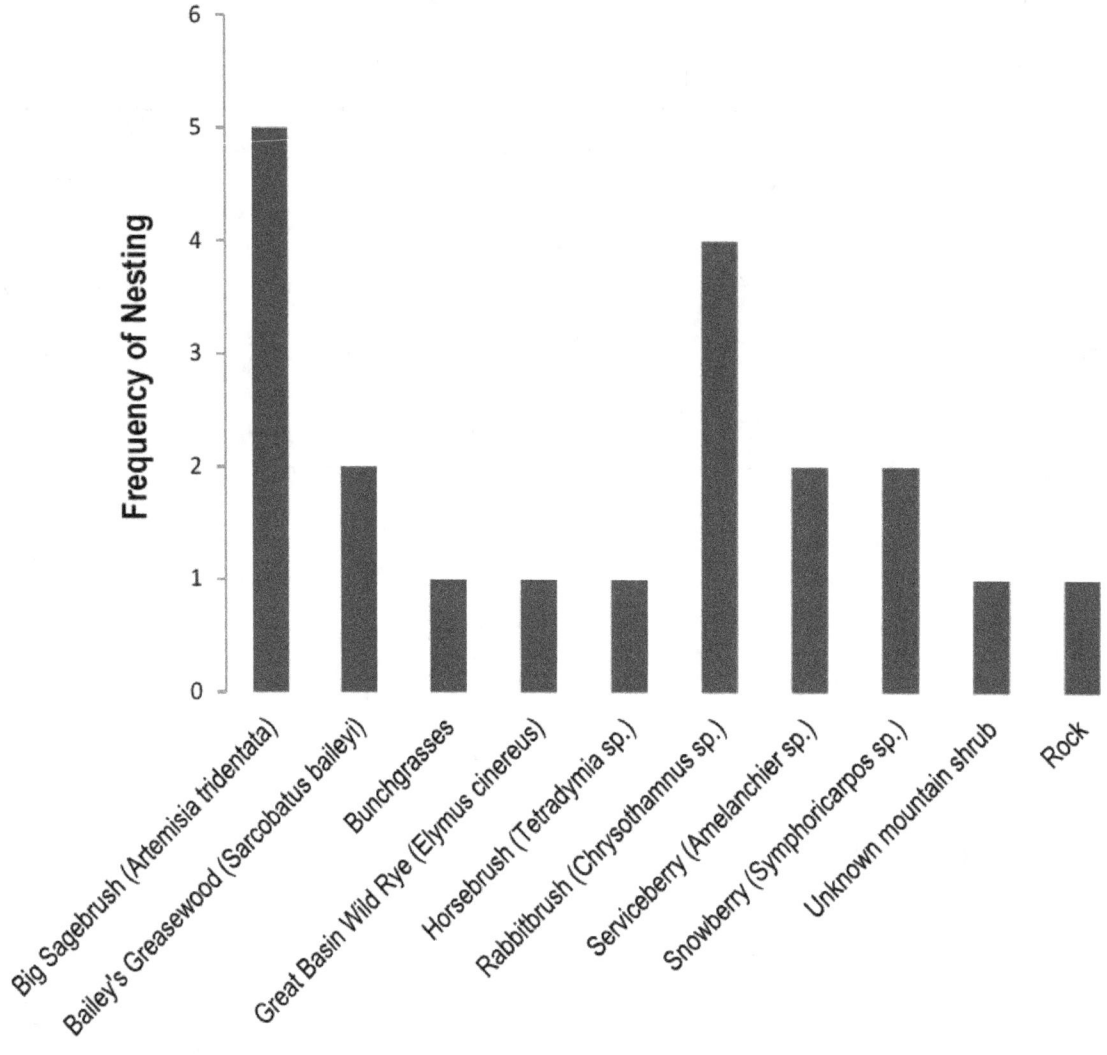

Figure 8. Frequency of use of overhead cover type of sage-grouse nests in the Virginia Mountains during 2009 and 2010.

Our preliminary results suggest sage-grouse did not select areas with greater sagebrush cover (fig. 9), even though sagebrush was often selected as the nesting shrub; however, other species of shrub appeared to be selected by sage-grouse (fig. 9). The percentage of sagebrush cover remained relatively consistent as the distance from the nest increased. The average sagebrush cover was 1.6 ± 0.07 percent (fig. 9). Of the total cover within 100 m of nests, 12.4 ± 0.6 percent was comprised of sagebrush species and 87.6 percent was nonsagebrush species. In comparing nest locations with random dependent locations (within 500 m from nests), 21 ± 10.3 percent more sagebrush was available at random locations than was used by sage-grouse. In comparing nest locations with random independent locations (those at the study site level), 48.5 ± 12.0 percent more sagebrush was available than was used by sage-grouse.

Our preliminary results suggest females select perennial grass for their nest sites, while avoiding annual grasses, especially cheatgrass, at proximities of 10 m or less from the nest (fig. 10). This effect was reduced at a distance of 25 m from the nest. When comparing the available habitat points, we found evidence for cheatgrass avoidance at both spatial scales (dependent and independent) within 10 m. The dependent random points had similar percentages of cover by perennial grass (12.6 ± 4.6 percent) as the area selected for nesting by sage-grouse (13.4 ± 2.5 percent); however, less perennial grass occurred at the independent location (8.6 ± 2.4 percent; availability at the study site level) compared to the used location within 10 m. Female sage-grouse did not appear to select for nest sites with more or less annual or perennial forbs (fig. 11).

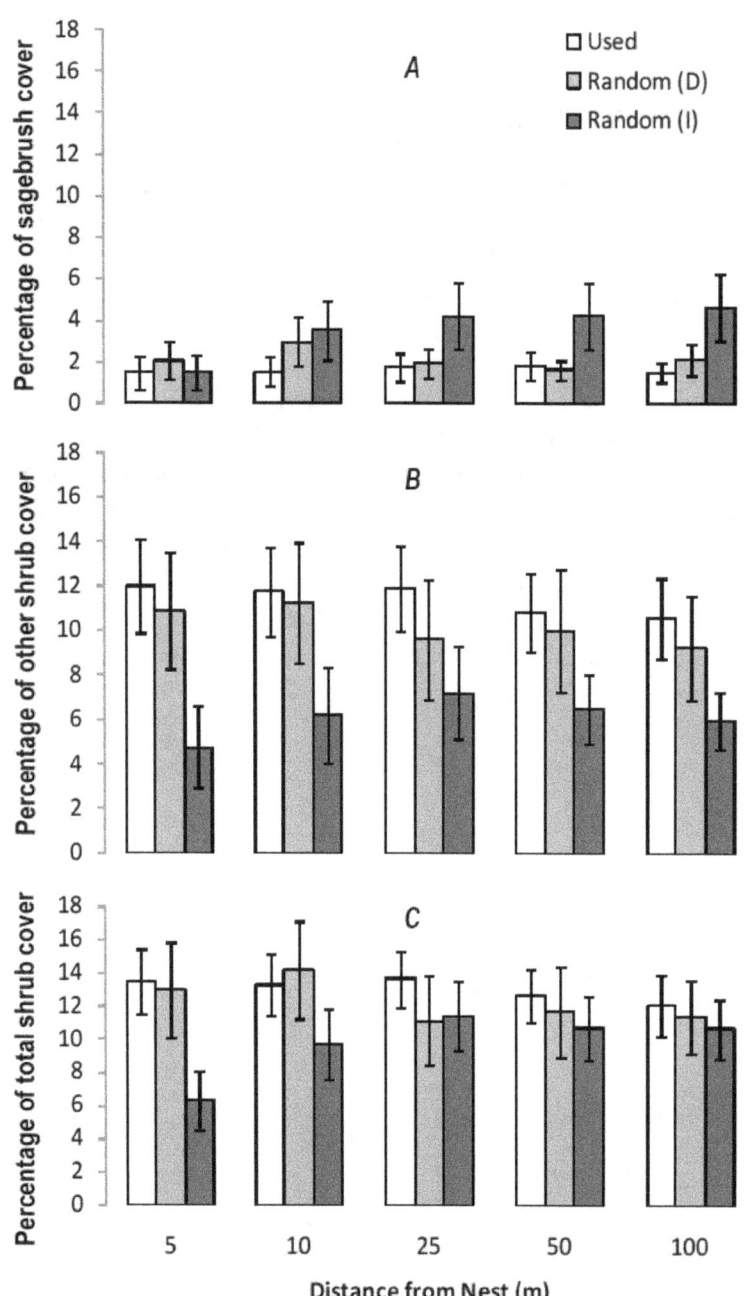

Figure 9. Mean values (lines represent standard errors) of percentages of cover by shrub types at 5, 10, 25, 50, and 100-m distances from nest sites and random locations. *A*, Sagebrush (*Artemisia* spp.). *B*, Other shrubs. *C*, Total shrubs. Percentage of cover was cumulative with an increase in distance.

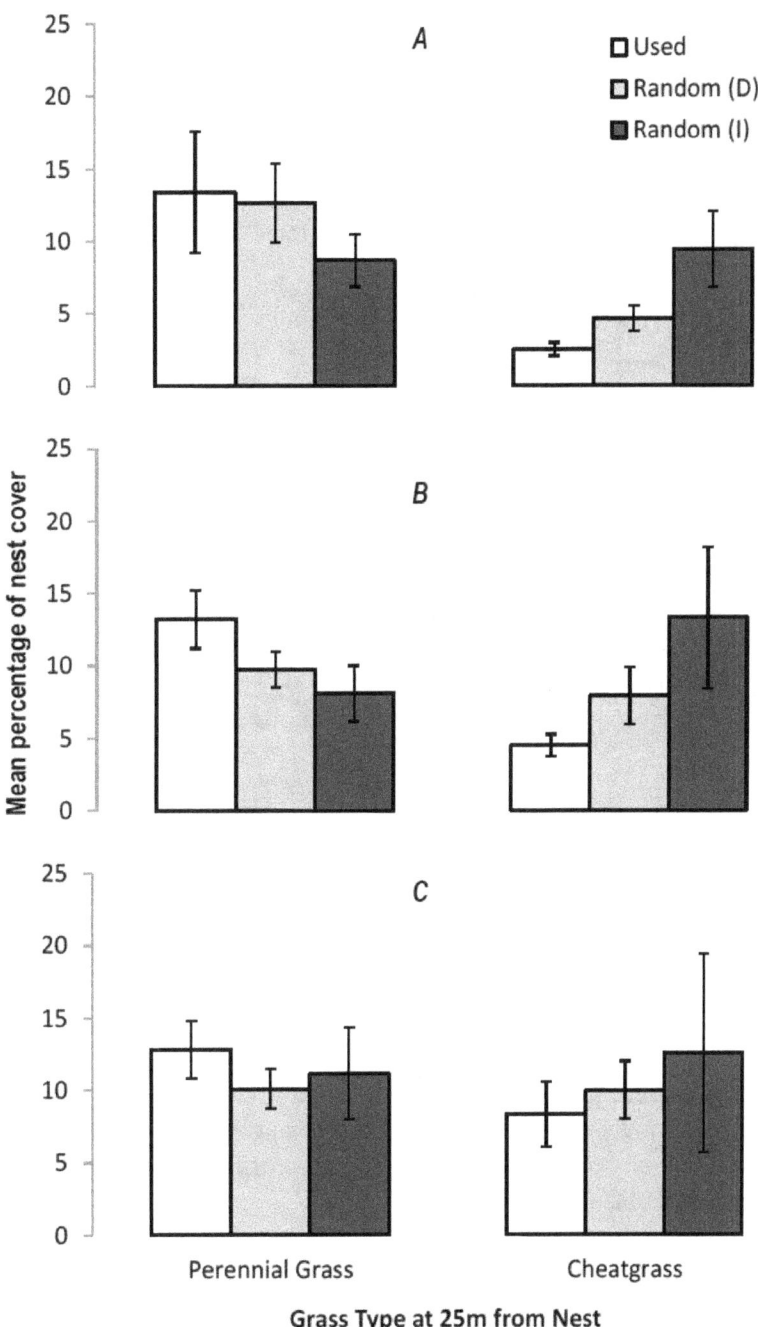

Figure 10. Mean values (lines represent standard errors) of percentages of cover by perennial grass and cheatgrass (*Bromus tectorum*) at nest sites compared to dependent and independent random points. *A*, Cover values around the nest. *B*, Cover values at 10 m from the nest. *C*, Cover values at 25 m from the nest.

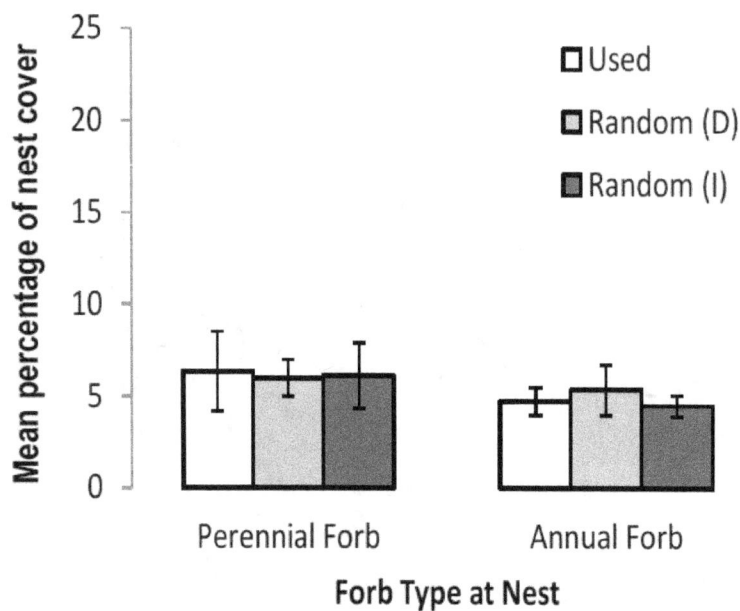

Figure 11. Mean values (lines represent standard errors) for percentages of cover by perennial and annual forbs at nest sites, nest-dependent random points, and nest-independent random points in the Virginia Mountains during 2009 and 2010.

Sage-Grouse Nest Videography

Twenty-two nests were video-monitored during 2009 (n = 6) and 2010 (n = 16). Four ravens, two badgers, two coyotes (*Canis latrans*), and one bobcat (*Lynx rufus*) were identified depredating nests by videography (n = 9; figs. 12 and 13).

Ravens

We captured four raven predations on video during daylight hours. Sage-grouse usually were flushed during these events. On one occasion, an incubating sage-grouse was attacked. Nest defense by each female sage-grouse was unsuccessful, and all eggs were either directly destroyed by ravens or abandoned after the event took place.

Badger, Coyote, and Bobcat

Badgers were responsible for one nest predation each year of the study. The two coyote and the single bobcat predation occurred in 2010, and all three of these predators depredated sage-grouse nests during night hours.

Weasel

We have no records of a successful predation by long-tailed weasels (*Mustela frenata*); however, on one night, a weasel attacked a female sage-grouse while her nest was hatching. Although the female sage-grouse tried to defend the eggs, all unhatched eggs were destroyed. The female sage-grouse fled with one chick that ultimately survived. The weasel was not subsequently observed eating or removing eggs or chicks from the nest it had originally attempted to depredate (USGS unpublished data).

Gopher Snake

We observed no successful egg predation events by snakes. In 2009, one relatively large gopher snake (*Pituophis catenifer*) was documented unsuccessfully attempting to swallow a sage-grouse egg for more than two hours. Another snake successfully captured and consumed a single hatched chick in a nest bowl. In this instance, the female sage-grouse left the nest with multiple chicks and did not return.

Ground Squirrel

California ground squirrels (*Spermophilus beecheyi*) have been the only species of squirrel to visit sage-grouse nests at the study area, and none have successfully depredated eggs. A ground squirrel was documented at a nest following a raven predation. The squirrel entered the nest bowl approximately ten hours after the female sage-grouse was flushed by the raven. Several minutes passed while the squirrel unsuccessfully attempted to bite into the egg. It appeared that the squirrel was limited by the width of its gape. One squirrel appeared to incidentally break open an egg after lifting and dropping it, at which time the squirrel consumed the egg's content. We have not documented rodents capable of flushing sage-grouse from their nests and consider the incidental egg breaking by the California ground squirrel a rare occurrence.

Hatches

Ten successful nest hatches were captured on video.

Abandonments

We recorded three nest abandonments. One abandonment appeared to be related to an injury to the wing of the incubating female. During maintenance visit to the nest to replace batteries and a memory card, the female sage-grouse was observed falling out of flight with an apparent injured wing. We recaptured the bird and discovered a broken or dislocated left humerus with collision abrasion to the wing. The injury showed evidence of collision with a metal structure and was not consistent with any known predator attack pattern of damage. We suspect the female collided with a guy-wire or post from the nearby meteorological tower (which happened to be within 200 m of her nest) because this anthropogenic structure was the only proximate tall structure capable of internal and external tissue damage. Following release, video monitoring documented the female frequenting the nest with irregular incubation recesses. She laid 9 eggs but eventually abandoned the nest. The sage-grouse was not capable of flight, and an unknown predator killed and consumed her within 21 days of injury. Another occurrence of abandonment appeared to be related to adverse weather conditions where snowfall buried the female and she subsequently abandoned her nest. The reason for the third nest abandonment was unknown.

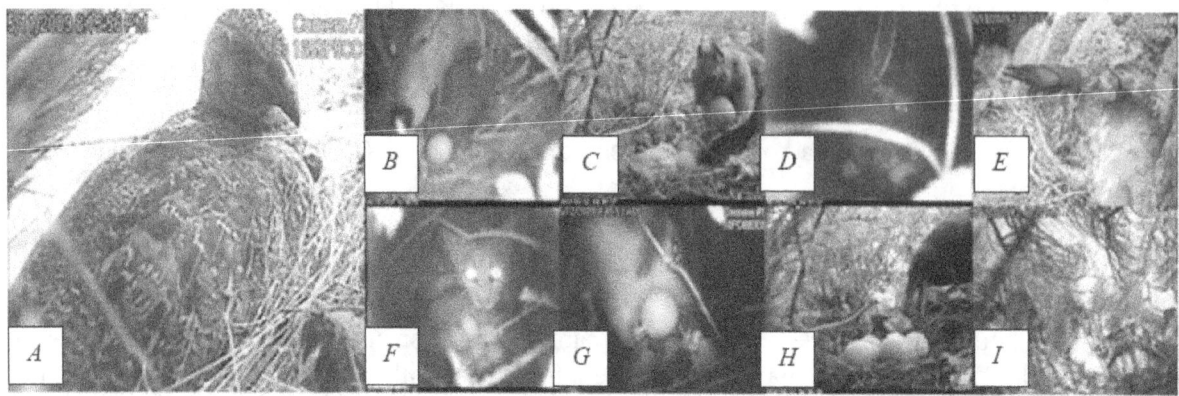

Figure 12. Images of nest activities at eight sage-grouse nests and one raven nest in the Virginia Mountains of northwestern Nevada during 2009 and 2010. *A*, A female sage-grouse incubating. *B*, A coyote depredating a nest. *C*, A California ground squirrel manipulating an egg after a raven predation. *D*, A weasel that attacked sage-grouse. *E*, A raven feeding her young. *F*, A bobcat depredating a nest. *G*, A badger depredating a nest. *H*, A raven depredating a nest. *I*, An unsuccessful attempt by a gopher snake to consume eggs.

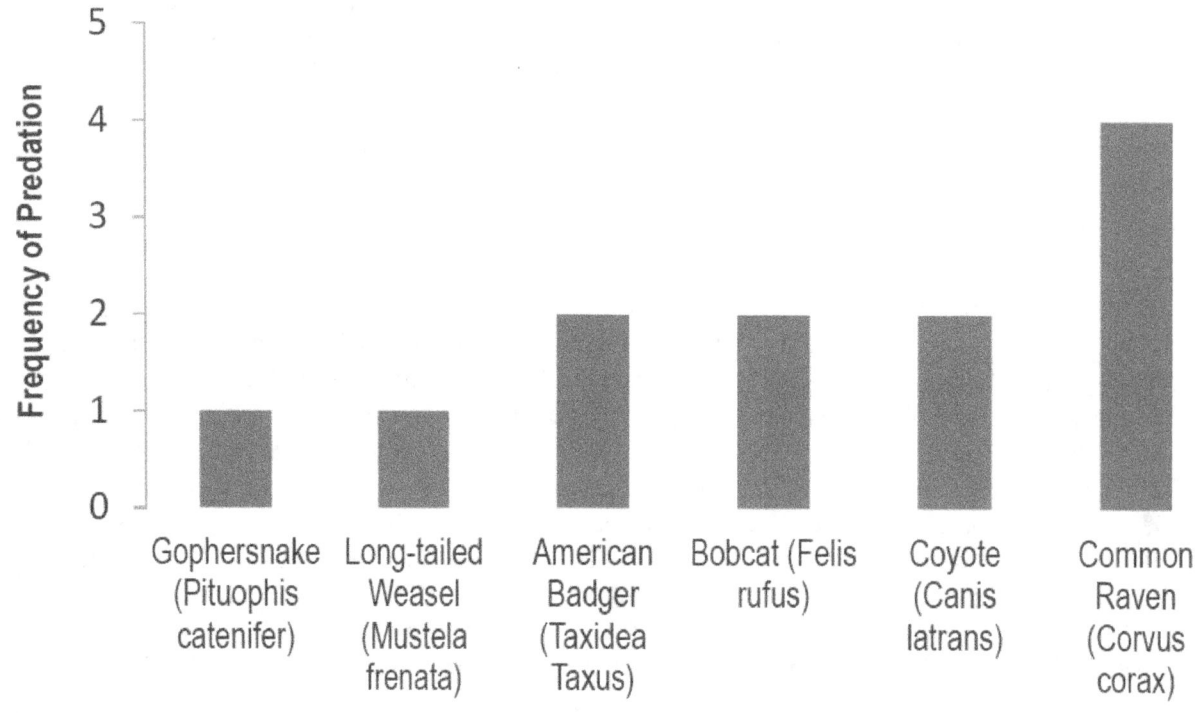

Figure 13. Frequency of documented encounters of species at sage-grouse nests in the Virginia Mountains during 2009 and 2010.

Figure 14. Sequence of still photographs from video recordings of a raven attacking a female sage-grouse and depredating the eggs within an 8-second period. *A,* The female incubating prior to being struck by the raven. *B,* Harassment of the sage-grouse by the raven. *C* and *D,* Female sage-grouse fleeing the nest. *E* and *F,* The raven depredating the eggs.

Brood Success

Brood success was defined by one chick or more alive at 50 days post-hatch. In 2009, brood success was 100 percent (at 50 days). We observed a female mortality with a brood prior to 30 days post-hatch in 2009 (unknown brood outcome). Of the nine broods in 2010, one failed by 40 days and 2 failed by 50 days post-hatch.

In both years, female sage-grouse moved with their broods to the higher elevations (often ridge tops) than during the nesting period. Those sites were generally characterized by relatively less grass and shrub canopy cover. During late July of both years, we observed females joining other sage-grouse where brood mixing occurred. Groups sometimes consisted of more than 20 individuals. Once female sage-grouse were in larger groups, it was often challenging to obtain chick counts for distinct females. During 2010, broods moved 455 ± 146.7 m between day and night observations that were conducted within a 24-hour interval (n = 23). In one instance, a female sage-grouse and her brood were found during the night at a location 3.6 km away from the daytime location.

Selection of Brood-Rearing Habitat

Our preliminary results showed evidence of selection for perennial forbs (used = 16.5 ± 1.5 percent; random = 10.9 ± 1.8 percent) but no selection for annual forbs (used = 5.6 ± 0.4 percent; random = 5.6 ± 0.5 percent). We also found some evidence of selection for perennial grass (used = 10.3 ± 1.2 percent; random = 8.4 ± 1.2 percent). Brood-rearing females did not appear to avoid cheatgrass (used = 6.6 ± 1.3 percent, random = 6.6 ± 1.6 percent), as they did during the nesting period (fig. 15).

Brood-rearing sage-grouse selected areas with greater vertical cover, measured by the cover board, than would be expected to occur at random points (fig. 16); however, sage-grouse did not appear to select areas with greater horizontal cover, measured by sagebrush canopy, through time (fig. 17). The random surveys indicate that sagebrush was available in areas where broods were located, yet sage-grouse appeared to not use areas of greater sagebrush cover. We found that shrub cover other than sagebrush was selected during the day (foraging) but not during the night (roosting; fig. 17). Brood day locations had 99.6 percent more total shrub-canopy cover than did brood night locations.

The relationship between day and night canopy cover and the species composition of vegetation appeared consistent throughout the 50-day post-hatching interval (fig. 17). It appeared that at 50 days, when the chicks from broods are relatively large and capable of sustained flight, less shrub cover was selected in daytime relative to what was available. The variation was relatively greater for samples at 50 days than at earlier intervals.

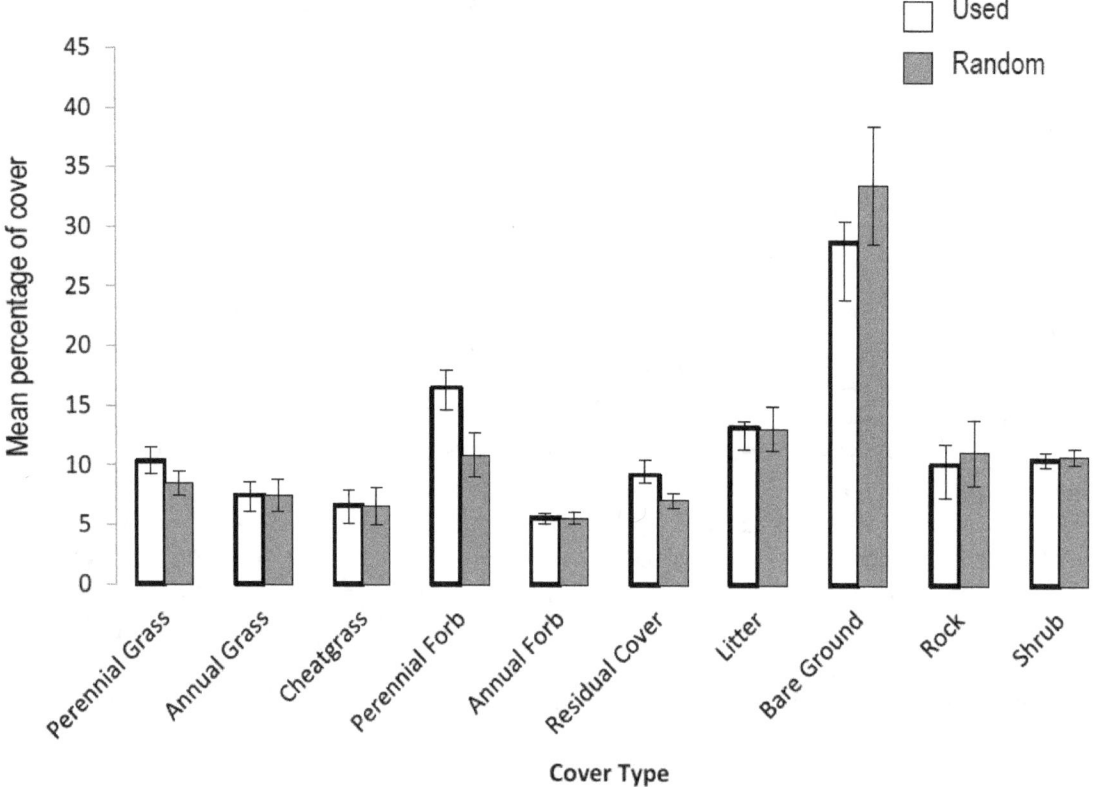

Figure 15. Mean values (lines represent standard errors) for percentages of cover types used by brood-rearing female sage-grouse and cover types found at brood-dependent random points.

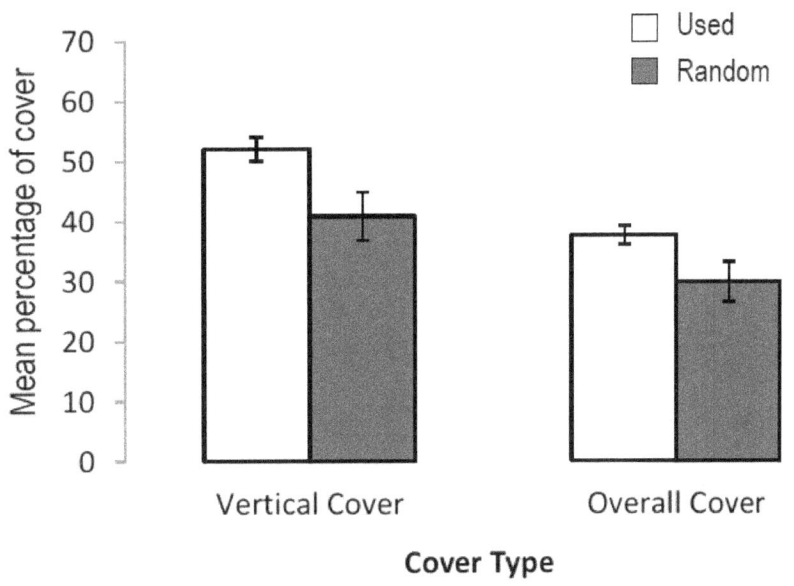

Figure 16. Mean values (lines represent standard errors) of percentages of vertical and overall cover for brood locations (open bars) and brood-dependent random locations (dark bars).

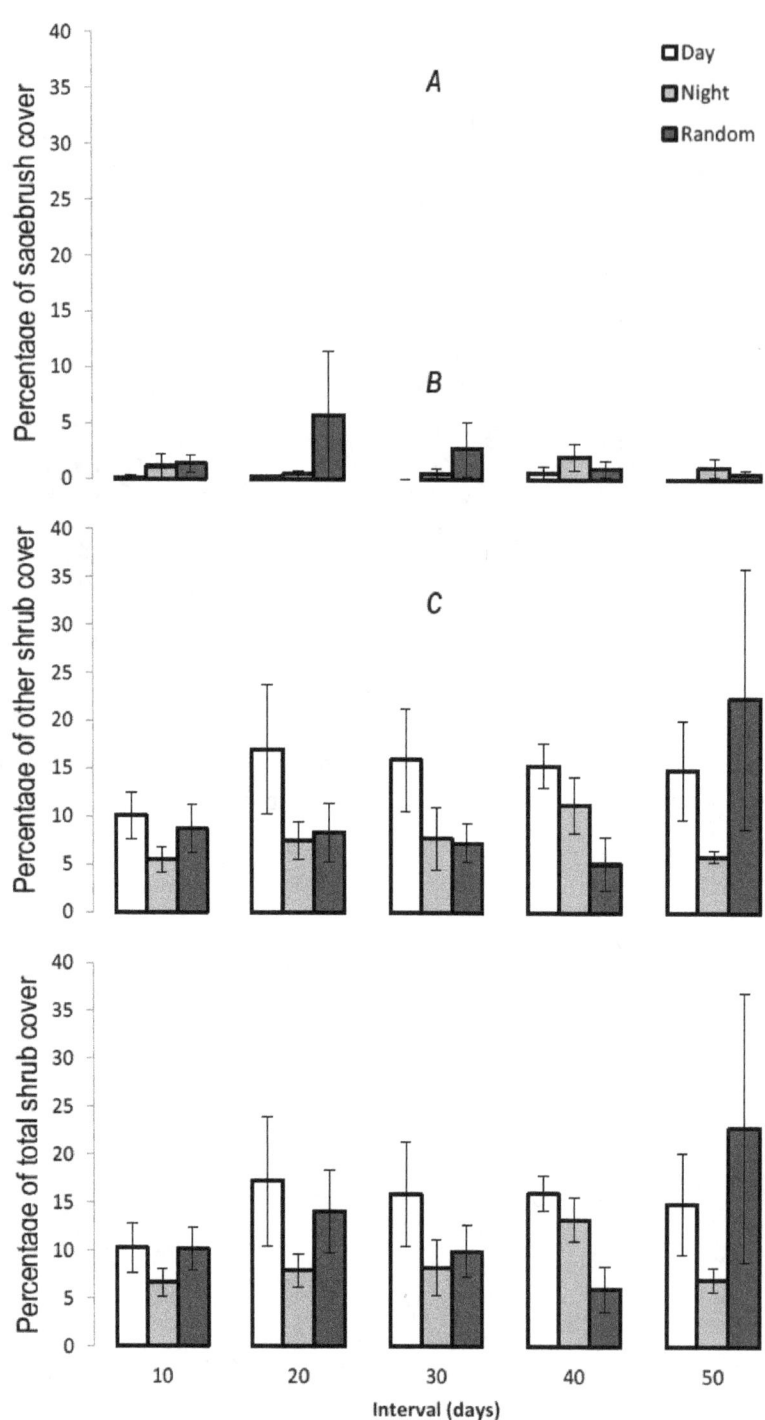

Figure 17. Percentages of cover (lines represent standard errors of the means) at day-nesting, night-nesting, and brood-dependent random locations over the 50-day post-hatch interval for sage-grouse in the Virginia Mountains during 2009 and 2010. *A*, Percentage of cover by sagebrush (*Artemisia tridentata*). *B*, Percentage of cover by other shrub types. *C*, Percentage of cover by all shrubs.

Predator Surveys

Data from point surveys for ravens and raptors and transect surveys for badger activity will be compiled upon completion of the study. Predator abundance indices will be used as covariates in nest and brood survival models, allowing us to explore explained variation by these factors on vital rates of sage-grouse in the Virginia Mountains. We also will investigate the probability of nests depredated by each species of predator based on microhabitat characteristics. We have completed 99 surveys (badger, raven, and raptor) at sage-grouse nests. We have also completed over 500 random surveys of ravens and raptors throughout the study area (fig. 18).

We installed cameras on three raven nests in the northern portion of the study site during 2009 (n=2) and 2010 (n=1). In 2009, one of the nests was located in a natural cliff structure, while the other nest was positioned on an electrical transmission pole along Fish Springs Road. The following year, we reinstalled a camera on the nest positioned on the transmission pole. Personnel from Nevada Energy assisted us with the installation of the camera and digital video recorder (DVR) system. We collected approximately 2,500 hours of continuous videography on raven behaviors such as, chick feeding and adult feeding times, chick provisioning rates, and general activity during sage-grouse nesting periods. We obtained clear images of feeding (fig. 20), and we plan to quantify the amount of raven diet that consists of avian items (e.g., evidence of egg or chicks) throughout the sage-grouse nesting period.

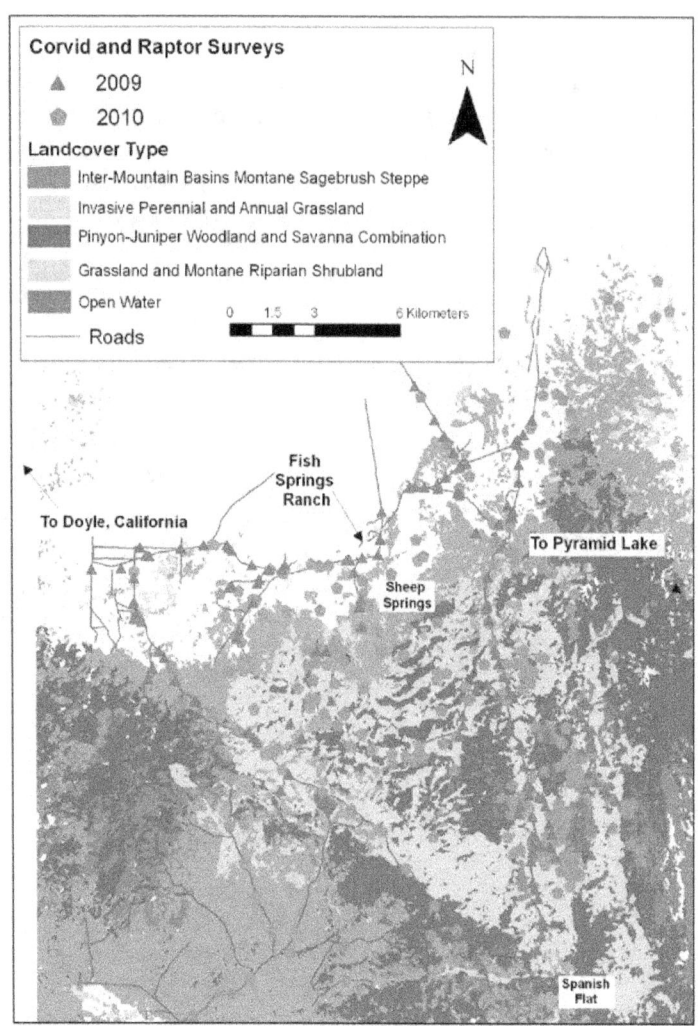

Figure 18. Distribution of point surveys for ravens and raptors across the study areas in the Virginia Mountains of Nevada during 2009 and 2010.

 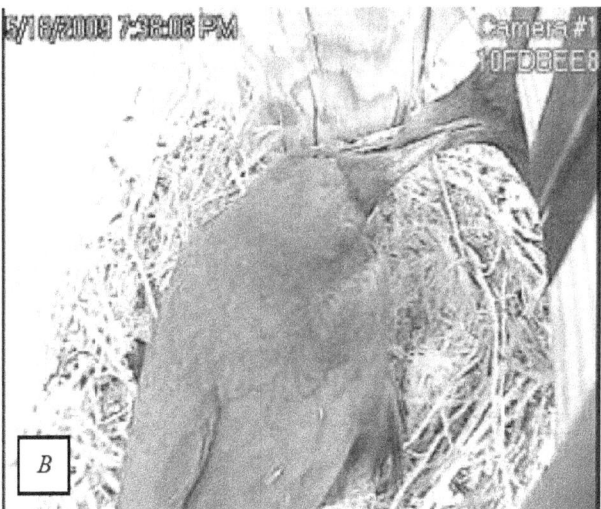

Figure 19. Raven nests monitored in 2009. *A,* An adult returns to feed nestlings at a nest located on a cliff ledge. *B,* Adults exchanging food to pass to nestlings in a next located on a transmission pole.

Preliminary Data Interpretation

Growth and maintenance of sage-grouse populations in the Virginia Mountains study area appear limited and, based on preliminary findings, may be the result of relatively low nest survival. Range-wide averages of nest success (~ 50 percent; Schroeder and others, 1999) were substantially greater than estimates for the Virginia Mountains (13 percent). Although most studies across sage-grouse range reported apparent nest success rates, which overestimate nest survival (Kolada and others, 2009; Coates and Delehanty, 2010), sage-grouse nest survival in the Virginia Mountains was substantially lower than in other areas of Nevada (Kolada and others, 2009; Coates and Delehanty, 2010). Our limited sample size indicates that estimated brood success, in contrast to other populations within these study years, was relatively high compared to range-wide values (Schroeder and others, 1999).

Increased wildfire cycles, coupled with increased seed production of cheatgrass, often result in invasive grass replacing intact sagebrush steppe across the landscape (Brooks and Pyke, 2001). At our study site, the majority of cheatgrass grew at relatively high elevations and sagebrush steppe was still relatively intact at lower elevations. Sage-grouse appeared to select nesting areas that were not within the lower elevation areas but instead selected nesting areas on greater slopes at relatively high elevations. Although sage-grouse appeared to avoid areas with cheatgrass, cover in these areas still largely consisted of this invasive plant species, which does not appear to provide the cover necessary for concealment for successful nesting.

One explanation for why sage-grouse appear to nest at higher elevation sites with greater invasive grasses and much less shrub cover is site fidelity. Because of rapid invasion by cheatgrass based on increasing fire cycles, behavioral adjustment by sage-grouse may not correspond to the rapid changes in landscape vegetation. In other words, sage-grouse may have nested at the higher elevations prior to cheatgrass invasion and still maintain general nesting areas, even though habitat quality has deteriorated. Another explanation is that higher elevation sites offer other important factors necessary for reproduction, such as proximity to upland springs for broods and greater distance from urban expansion at lower elevations. Sage-grouse may be avoiding nest predators often associated with anthropogenic structures (for example, roads and transmission lines). By positioning nests at relatively high elevations, females will be closer to open areas for brood-rearing. For example, we found females with broods appear to roost at night in relatively high elevation open areas without dense shrub cover, possibly where they can easily escape terrestrial predators by taking flight. However, we found during daylight hours, they moved their broods to areas with greater cover, which may provide more abundant food sources (for example, insects and forbs) and concealment.

These hypotheses are not mutually exclusive. The benefits of predator avoidance while positioning nests in areas with access to upland springs for foraging and brood rearing following hatch may outweigh costs associated with loss of nesting cover at higher elevations. As we collect additional data, we will be able to assess the influence of the invasive annual grasses on habitat selection for nest sites by sage-grouse.

Raven populations appear relatively high throughout the study area compared to other reported numbers in Nevada sagebrush ecosystems (Coates and Delehanty, 2010). Ravens select powerlines for perching and nesting compared to other natural features (for example, cliff and tree) in the environment (Knight and Kawashima, 1993), and we observed ravens using anthropogenic structures at our study area. Raven abundance is negatively correlated with sage-grouse nest survival (Bui and others, 2010; Coates and Delehanty, 2010). Therefore, based on these preliminary findings and other studies, development of anthropogenic infrastructure within the Spanish Flat area of the Virginia Mountains may further reduce sage-grouse nest survival rates, especially with lack of nesting vegetation cover associated with increased cheatgrass invasion.

With additional observations in the field, we will estimate nest, brood, and adult survival as a function of habitat factors and predator indices. We will also model movement across the landscape in relation to larger scale vegetation characteristics (for example, annual grass-cover types) and topography (for example, elevation and slope). Subsequent to energy development in this region, we will include energy-related covariates (for example, distance to transmission line) to inform movement and vital rate models.

These reported data represent preliminary findings. Further study of nest predators, habitat, and energy development is required before conclusions can be made about the Virginia Mountain population of sage-grouse. This type of study that focuses on measurements taken before and after energy development can provide critical information necessary to guide energy development in sagebrush ecosystems and, if needed, to mitigate potential negative effects to sage-grouse populations.

Acknowledgments

This report was prepared for the Nevada Department of Wildlife under agreement No. 09-52 with the U.S. Geological Survey. Nevada Department of Wildlife and U.S. Fish and Wildlife Service provided funding to support this research. Sage-grouse were handled in accordance with the Animal Care and Use Committee, Western Ecological Research Center, with review from the University of California-Davis Wildlife Health Center.

We thank Chris Hampson with the Nevada Department of Wildlife for logistical support Rosemary Smith with the Idaho State University provided additional advice on study design and interpretation of results.

We thank Jonathan Dudko, Nick Kelly, Brian Halstead, and Pamela Gore with the U. S. Geological Survey for their substantial contributions in the field and office.

Literature Cited

Ammann, G.A., 1944, Determining the age of pinnated and sharp-tailed grouse: Journal of Wildlife Management, v. 8, p.170–171.

Anderson, D.R., 2008, Model based inference in the life sciences: New York, N.Y., Springer Science, 184 p.

Beyer, H.L., 2004, Hawth's Analysis Tools for ArcGIS. Accessed April 18, 2011 at *http://www.spatialecology.com/htools.*.

Boarman, W.I., 2003, Managing a subsidized predator population—Reducing common raven predation on desert tortoises: Environmental Management, v. 32, p. 205–217.

Brooks, M.L., and Pyke, D.A., 2000, Invasive plants and fire in the deserts of North America, *in* Galley, K.E.M, and Wilson, T.P., eds., Proceedings of the Invasive Species Workshop—The role of fire in the control and spread of invasive species, Fire Conference 2000—The First National Congress on Fire Ecology, Prevention, and Management: Tall Timbers Research Station, Tallahassee, Fla., Miscellaneous Publication No 11, p. 1–14.

Bui, T.D., Marzluff, J.M., and Bedrosian, Bryan., 2010, Common Raven activity in relation to land use in western Wyoming—Implications for Greater Sage-Grouse reproductive success: The Condor, v, 112, p. 65–78.

Casazza, M.L., Coates, P.S., and Overton, C.T, in press, Linking habitat selection to brood success in greater sage-grouse—A multi-scale modeling approach: Studies in Avian Biology.

Coates, P.S., and Delehanty, D.J., 2008, Effects of environmental factors on incubation patterns of greater sage-grouse: The Condor, v. 110, p. 627–638.

Coates, P.S., Connelly, J.W., and Delehanty, D.J., 2008, Predators of greater sage-grouse nests identified by video monitoring: Journal of Field Ornithology, v. 79, p. 421–428.

Coates, P.S., and Delehanty, D.J., 2010, Nest predation of greater sage-grouse in relation to microhabitat factors and predators: Journal of Wildlife Management, v. 74, p. 240–248.

Daubenmire, R.F., 1959, A canopy-coverage method of vegetation analysis: Northwest Science, v. 33, p. 43–66.

Hall, L.S., Krausman, P.R., and. Morrison, M.L., 1997, The habitat concept and a plea for standard terminology: Wildlife Society Bulletin, v. 25, p. 173–182.

Holloran, M.J., and Anderson, S.H., 2003, Direct identification of northern sage-grouse, *Centrocercus urophasianus*, nest predators using remote sensing cameras: The Canadian Field-Naturalist, v. 117, p. 308–310.

Horne, J.S., and Garton, E.O., 2009, Animal Space Use 1.3 [software, beta test version]: Moscow, Idaho, University of Idaho, College of Natural Resources, Dr. Edward O. Garton Web page, accessed August 6, 2010, at *http://www.cnr.uidaho.edu/population_ecology/animal_space_use.htm*.

Jones, R.E., 1968, A board to measure cover used by prairie grouse: Journal of Wildlife Management, v. 32, p. 28–31.

Knight, R.L., and Kawashima, J.Y., 1993, Responses of raven and red-tailed hawk populations to linear right-of-ways: Journal of Wildlife Management, v. 57, p. 266–271.

Kolada, E.J., Casazza, M.L., and Sedinger, J.S., 2009, Ecological factors influencing nest survival of greater sage-grouse in Mono County, California: Journal of Wildlife Management, v. 73, p. 1341–1347.

Laake, J., and E. Rexstad, 2007, RMark—an alternative approach to building linear models. In Appendix C *in* Cooch, E., and G. White, eds., Program MARK: a gentle introduction. Accessed July 11, 2011 at *http://www.phidot.org/software/mark/docs/book/*.

Manly, F.J., McDonald, L.L., Thomas, D.L., McDonald, T.L., and Erickson, W.P., 2002, Resource selection by animals—Statistical design and analysis for field studies: London, Chapman and Hall, 240 p.

Moynahan, B.J., Lindberg, M.S., and Thomas, J.W., 2006, Factors contributing to process variance in annual survival of female greater sage-grouse in Montana: Ecological Applications, v. 16, p. 1529–1538.

Robel, R.J., Briggs, J.N., Dayton, A.D., and Hulbert, L.C., 1970, Relationship between visual obstruction measurements and weight of grassland: Journal of Range Management, v. 23, p. 295–297.

Schroeder, M.A., Young, J.R., and Braun, C.E., 1999, Greater sage-grouse (*Centrocercus urophasianus*), *in* Poole, A., ed., The birds of North America online, no. 425: Ithaca, N.Y., Cornell Lab of Ornithology, accessed April 18, 2011, at *http://bna.birds.cornell.edu/bna/species/425*.

Thomas, L., Buckland, S.T., Rexstad, E.A., Laake, J.L., Strindberg, S., Hedley, S.L., Bishop, J.R.B., Marques, T.A., and Burnham, K.P., 2010, Distance software: Design and analysis of distance sampling surveys for estimating population size: Journal of Applied Ecology, v. 47, p. 5–14.

Wakkinen, W.L., Reese, K.P., Connelly, J.W., and Fischer, R.A., 1992, An improved spotlighting technique for capturing sage grouse: Wildlife Society Bulletin, v. 20, p. 425–426.

Worton, B.J., 1989, Kernel methods for estimating the utilization distribution in home-range studies: Ecology, v. 70, p. 164–168.

www.ingramcontent.com/pod-product-compliance
Lightning Source LLC
Chambersburg PA
CBHW080350290526
45791CB00009BA/2814